THE COLORFUL WORLD OF BUTTONS

by Viviane Beck Ertell

THE PYNE PRESS PRINCETON

Library of Congress Catalog Card Number 72–95724

SBN 87861–037–5

Printed in the United States of America

The Colorful World of Buttons

To the wonderful
times
George and I had collecting

LIST OF PLATES

PREFACE

The Colorful World of Buttons by Viviane Beck Ertell is a unique book in intent, content and treatment of the subject matter. It introduces the reader to one of the world's great private collections, a dazzling array which includes outstanding examples in nearly all categories. In the summer of 1972 this collection was given a permanent public home, the Viviane Beck Ertell Button Museum, at Liberty Village, Flemington, New Jersey. And now with The Colorful World of Buttons, Mrs. Ertell has sought to share her expertise and good fortune with an even wider audience.

Here is represented the finest work of the button maker, produced from any material you can imagine, including precious gems set in gleaming gold, miniatures painted on ivory and delicately shaded Wedgwood plaques—these from the eighteenth century. From the nineteenth century are the ever-present and interesting black glass buttons and those pressed from the lowly animal horn and hoof. There is also a representative showing of twentieth century buttons, manufactured in a great variety of modern plastics, some of which have been formed in realistic shapes.

The hundreds of buttons on 43 plates are shown in their original colors. This is a great advantage to the collector, for as is well known in collecting circles, the more thoroughly you know an object, the more likely you are to find it or a similar one. Another important feature of this book is that many of the individual buttons are described as to material and technique; this factor, together with the full-color likeness, provides the collector with a very precise idea of the object's historical and physical identity. The fact that political campaign buttons and those used on uniforms are not included does not detract from the overall usefulness and value of this book. These categories of collecting are highly specialized, and definitive works are already available for those who need them.

Button collecting, as a recognized hobby, started in 1938, with the formation of The National Button Society. With the help of the official publication, The National Button Bulletin, button collecting has advanced to the point where it is considered the most popular hobby, after stamp and coin collecting. The National Button Society has already issued individual booklets on such classifications of the more popular and plentiful buttons as black glass, clear and colored glass, china, and those of pearl and shell. Although it is true that some of the buttons shown in this volume are not readily available to the average collector, it is possible for the active collector to obtain many of the specimens that are illustrated. The many different categories presented in *The Colorful World of Buttons* are evidence of the degree of specialization which has occurred in recent years. A study of the frames of buttons on exhibition at any button meeting reveals that collectors are now concentrating in several fields, notably enamels, minature paper-weights, lacy glass, carved pearls, picture and story buttons. The illustrations of these buttons are a valuable aid to anyone preparing a collection in any one of the popular categories.

Viviane Beck Ertell is well known in the button-collecting world, both here in the United States and abroad. Although not a charter member of The National Button Society, she has been an active member, as well as a dealer, for many years. Her late husband, George Ertell, served successively as vice-president, president and member of the board of directors of the national organization over a period of seven years. Viviane and George Ertell attended the annual national meetings, as well as many of the state society gatherings in all parts of the country.

The Ertells brought to America one of the most important and valuable European collections of button materials, the famed D'Allemagne Collection of Paris. This comprehensive collection is well represented and richly illustrated in these pages. Also, the Ertells were instrumental in the distribution of the sample books of the oldest button manufacturing company in the world, Firmins of London—the books which provide so much important documentary evidence of the development of styles and forms. With a number of these books in hand, George Ertell became intrigued with the heraldic devices on the coat-of-arms and crest buttons of old British families. After considerable research, he contributed a series of articles to *The National Button Bulletin* with identifications and illustrations of many such buttons worn by liveried employees.

Scores of old-time collectors will remember with pleasure the handsome slides which the Ertells shared with their fellow enthusiasts. George Ertell acquired expertise in photography and prepared hundreds of kodachrome views of choice buttons found not only in their collection, but also in such superb holdings as those of the City Museum of Birmingham, England, the Carnavalet in Paris, and the Cooper-Hewitt Museum in New York. Some of his finest slides carried views of buttons in the famous Hanna Sicher Kohn Collection in the Metropolitan Museum of Art, New York, including the delicate polychrome painting on ivory of Amelie, mounted in a beautiful gold openwork scalloped border, set alternately with forty genuine diamonds and rubies. Many collectors throughout the country received information and inspiration from the Ertells to improve their collections. *The Colorful World of Buttons* is a most appropriate tribute to the hobby and to two individuals who so advanced it.

Hightstown, New Jersey   ALPHAEUS H. ALBERT

INTRODUCTION

Over the years, many collectors of buttons approached my late husband, George Ertell, about writing a book on the rarest and most beautiful buttons of the eighteenth and nineteenth centuries. Certainly, he was well qualified by knowledge and experience to undertake such a work. Throughout the many years of our collecting, he had made color slides of most of my collection, and he had also been privileged to photograph the Hanna S. Kohn Collection, now in the Metropolitan Museum of Art, and the Hewitt and other collections, which are now in the Cooper-Hewitt Museum. He had thus amassed an outstanding permanent record of most of the fine buttons which have come to light since button collecting became an organized field of study. Unfortunately, despite the fact that the basic groundwork was already laid, Mr. Ertell had not begun actual work on the book until just before his death in March, 1967.

My original aim in compiling a book myself was simply to use the color slides he left to us, but in the course of several years preparatory investigations, this plan was found to be impracticable. However, so much thought and planning for that project had given me the impetus to consider doing a book about my collection: to have the finest buttons from my collection photographed in color and to provide a descriptive text to accompany the pictures.

Hence, it should be clear to my readers and my fellow collectors that I have no intention of issuing a textbook; several fine ones are already available. This book, then, is a record in color of the best from one collection of fine buttons, with a description of the materials and methods used in their crafting insofar as I am able to provide such information. Here and there, my analyses are hypothetical. As other researchers will understand, it is not always possible to find a broken or damaged button to examine in order to confirm our "guesses." Thus I cannot, in every instance, say with complete certainty of what material a button is made.

My efforts in this direction were much aided by the work of Lillian Smith Albert, who helped so many of us and the hobby itself. Much of the descriptive material in this book stems from her research, and I am of the opinion that she was the finest researcher the hobby has produced so far. We all have her to thank for so much of the accurate information extant concerning materials and techniques used in the making of buttons. We also acknowledge the fine scholarly work of Jane Ford Adams. With the passage of time, new facts will appear, and we shall have to change our judgments as to age and techniques and materials, but all this will be possible for us because of the work of these two ladies.

The buttons chosen for illustration in this book, however, were selected primarily for their beauty. Rare buttons are not axiomatically beautiful ones. The reader must not feel slighted if buttons similar to the choice ones in his or her collection are not represented here. Most of the buttons shown date from the eighteenth and early nineteenth centuries, the heyday of craftsmanship in so many areas of the applied arts. There are, certainly, some late nineteenth and early twentieth century buttons of great beauty and fine workmanship, too. Many buttons from more recent times are eminently collectible. Hence, buttons are displayed here that date from the seventeenth, eighteenth, nineteenth and twentieth centuries.

Perhaps buttons from the earlier times require some notes for proper orientation toward those eras. Seventeen color plates are devoted to the earlier buttons, and I have tried to choose buttons to cover most of the techniques used in those times. Most of the buttons were hand crafted, and many were made by famous artists of the period. A gentleman—for men wore the art-buttons then for the most part—ordering a new costume would commission an artist to execute a fine set of buttons to his own design or on a specified subject. The gentleman would also specify the materials. Dandies of the time actually vied with one another to sport the finest, most beautiful buttons. Neither the cost of the material nor the fee of the artist/craftsman was significant to these connoisseurs of the miniature arts, so that ivory, gold or jewels were in vogue from time to time. Miniatures were painted on ivory, carved and cut-out ivory, silk, paper, mica, pearl, porcelain and other materials. Other vogues prevailed, too. Colored foil was used in a number of ways, and painting or drawing with ink on the reverse side of the glass cover was very popular. The under-glass buttons of this period had copper or brass rims and tin backs. Paste jewels of the best quality appeared set in silver or gilt. Needlework was used extensively, with the same design appearing on buttons as on the gilet or coat they adorned. Inlay is found less frequently as is a silver-resist type of decoration on pearl. Less splendid outfits used buttons made of wood, bone, agate, hair, straw, and the like.

The subject matter of the painted pictures or embroidery on buttons was very varied, but certain scenes or motifs predominated in certain periods.

A technique that requires special mention is the "sulphides." These have been found mostly set in eighteenth century copper buttons. In *Connoisseur,* for April, 1954, Apsley Pellat is credited with making the button pictured there of a Spanish setter by Stubbs. This was part of Pellat's experimental work which produced a crystallo-ceramic technique he patented in the early nineteenth century. On Plate 14, button 12 has the same design. Crystal engraving with a composition (sulphide) fill is the technique used here as far as I can determine it.

"Colonials" are heavy metal buttons dating from the last part of the eighteenth century and into the early years of the nineteenth. They are chiefly English in origin, but some plain ones were found on the uniforms of German mercenaries of that period and some few were produced on this side of the Atlantic by at least one maker. We show some here on Plates 4, 5 and 6. Colonials were made of copper or brass, sometimes plated, with a heavy shank; most of them are flat and of sturdy construction. They have been found plain, engraved, die struck, chased, engine turned, and in combinations of these techniques. Those of complex construction are combined with enamel, glass, pearl, painting on ivory under glass, for examples. An overlay or inlay of another metal was frequently used, giving a two- or three-color effect. Some of the colonials are painted. These have survived least successfully, as the paint used was not durable. The exception was an imitation Wedgwood effect, accomplished on a molded center, with the background in blue enamel.

Mr. Ertell had acquired a sample case of "Fine Gilt Buttons," Colonials, made in Birmingham, England, and dated 1786. The case was in fine condition, and the 96 buttons like new.

Perhaps one collection within our collection merits a word about its provenance. The buttons shown in Plates 2, 3 and 4 represent the D'Allemagne Collection, the history of which may enhance them even more. Mr. Ertell liked to tell about our acquiring these magnificent buttons this way:

> Years ago when we first started to collect buttons we heard of the fabulous collection in Paris of M. H. R. D'Allemagne. Some of the finest items in the collection were recorded in his three-volume work, *Les Accessoires du Costume et du Mobilier.* It was the only record of fine buttons at that time, and the first time we went to Europe in search of buttons, we were urged by the late Lillian Smith Albert to try to see the collection. We finally contacted the family and were invited to their home. This was the beginning of an interesting friendship.
>
> Needless to say, we were thrilled by the quality and quantity as well as the wide variety of buttons. M. D'Allemagne was well advanced in years and not at all interested in disposing of any part of his extensive collections. He collected everything—the Paris house itself was a museum of the finest collectibles.
>
> Our friendship with the family continued, and one time when I arrived in Paris during the holiday season, I was informed that M. D'Allemagne had passed away on Christmas Day. I immediately called at their Paris residence to offer my condolences. The family maintained an apartment on the third story. I let myself into the bronze and

iron cage of the elevator, pressed the button, and, finally after a few vibrations, the elevator rose at a snail's pace. I found my friend, Jacques D'Allemagne, now the head of the family, nursing a case of the 'flu. Nevertheless, he insisted I visit with him. I must have been there two hours, and, as I was ready to leave, he stopped me and asked, "How would you like to buy my father's button collection?"

The next day I received a cable from my husband, asking me to deposit money to his account. He had never expected such an opportunity when he left for Paris, but he knew I would be pleased with this stroke of luck. Then he arranged for the shipment home of most of the collection, but the rarer items he brought back with him.

M. D'Allemagne had sewn hundreds of wood and some bone-back buttons as well as graduated sizes of steels on red-velvet-covered cardboards. When the shipment arrived, we went over these and many other types, joined by Mr. and Mrs. Alphaeus Albert (Lillian Smith Albert), who always came to see our new finds for research purposes. We all agreed that the buttons were splendid and that our acquisition represented a great stroke of fortune for ourselves and button collecting in this country, too. This small but important group, we hope, will always be kept intact. Collecting is full of travel and friends, luck and adventure—and disappointments, too.

Since this is a picture book, some further comments to the collector-reader may be in order. First, I hope you will find pleasure in looking through the history of buttons as represented in this collection, and that perhaps along the way, you may find you have a button like one pictured here. I have omitted many rare and important buttons such as horn, Goodyears, Jacksonians, Golden Ages, G. W.'s and others, because excellent books on these categories are already available as are also books on the technical aspects and the history of buttons. The plates may seem a little full in this book, but that makes possible showing even more buttons. Occasionally, there are pictured two, four or more buttons from a set. A full set from the eighteenth century may run to four or five dozen buttons, including those for the gilet, or vest, and breeches. Often in those times the buttons for a coat bore different designs, but all related to one subject.

Because this is a picture book in color, certain features will be emphasized, such as texture, depth, background material and other details which black and white reproduction cannot show. The buttons are shown in these pages at about 75 per cent of their actual size.

Since all the buttons shown are from my own collection, I cannot but hope that the reader will enjoy them, remembering that the book does represent, in the end, the efforts of so many persons who were our colleagues and our friends.

The Colorful World of Buttons

PLATE 1

Eighteenth Century Steel Buttons

This cartoon of an eighteenth-century dandy wearing steel buttons, made no doubt by Matthew Boulton of Birmingham, England, was published by H. Humphrey, Gerrard Street, Soho, London, on April 29, 1777. It was entitled "Steel Buttons. Coup de Bouton." As is clear enough from the picture, the brilliance of these steel buttons is dazzling to the lady.

2. The center top button has a pierced, sawtooth-edged pearl held to the basic button by a small round of steel, with both secured by a large steel pinshank.

7, 8, 11. Several of these buttons are pierced. Button 7, the center one on the right edge, is trimmed with balls that revolve.

STEEL BUTTONS. COUP DE BOUTON
Publd. 29 April, 1777, by H. Humphrey, Gerrard Street, Soho

1

PLATE 2

Eighteenth Century Soldiers

This set of buttons we considered one of the finest we had ever acquired. The groups of soldiers from the French Revolution are shown in different formations with assorted equipment. They are painted on opaline-like glass, bordered with fine twisted wires in a repeat design, with real seed pearls interspersed as decoration on the dark blue background, a *bleu-de-roi* glass.

This set of buttons is from the D'Allemagne Collection.

PLATE 3

Eighteenth Century Playing Cards

1, 2, 3, 4. The four ladies pictured at the top of this plate display the very decorative and ornate hats and coiffures of the late eighteenth century. The portraits are painted on paper and hand finished with color. They are set in brass collets.

5, 6, 7, 8. The next row consists of classical designs painted on ivory. The white border has begun to chip, and flakes of paint can easily be seen on the buttons. They are set in copper.

9 through 20. *Trompe l'oeil* was a popular form in the decorative arts toward the end of the eighteenth century, and was employed in decorating furniture, ceramics, boxes, trays and the like. These cards are painted on ivory. Set in brass and under glass.

These are all from the D'Allemagne Collection.

PLATE 4

Eighteenth Century: A Story Set
Some Colonials

I am sure the top twelve buttons tell a story. There must have been more buttons to the set, for there are gaps in the chronology. I read the story thus:

1. A little girl takes her first steps.

2. Mother and daughter go visiting.

3. The young girl is taught geography by her father.

4. She goes to her first ball.

5. She becomes engaged.

6. Her fiance celebrates before the wedding.

7. The wedding takes place.

8. Her husband says his farewells on going off to war.

9. Her husband reports for duty.

10. He goes forth into battle.

11. He is victorious.

12. He returns to his family.

13 through 24. The set below contains drawings in ink on paper of various activities, pleasures and occupations. Circa 1820.

Both of these sets are from the D'Allemagne Collection from France.

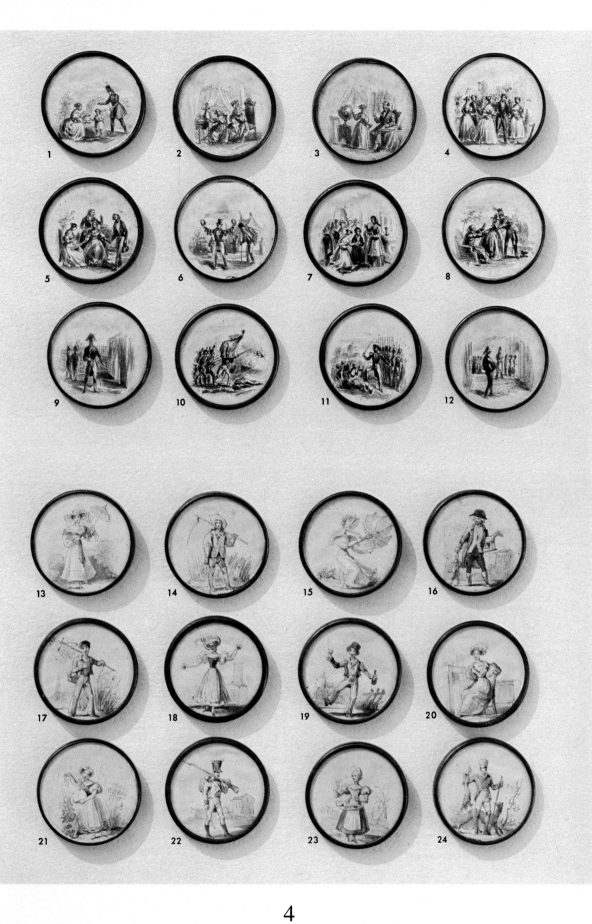

PLATE 5

Colonials

1.   Reverse painting on glass with chipped pearl in background.

2.   Engraved rim on a pinshanked agate.

3.   Pierrerie-trimmed pearl with a paste, or jewel, center, set on a plain surface with a punched edge. (Pierreries are tiny simulated gemstones much used in decorating buttons of the period.)

4 and 5.   Painted hunting scenes on glass set in a recessed well.

6.   Octagonal with opaline glass held in place with a metal pin.

7.   Beautiful pierced-brass trim set in a recessed well. Punched border.

8.   Another octagonal shape with a punched design.

9.   A painted ribbon design over an engine-turned and engraved base.

10.   A molded and punched trim design with enamel center.

11.   A classical figure with Wedgwood blue enamel painted background.

12.   Engine-turned and punched design.

13.   Reverse intaglio heads filled with a

sulphide material, with blue painted on the remainder of the glass. Border is a punched design.

14. Beautifully punched and engraved design of a flower.

15. Engraved flower with paint added.

16. Two-color metal.

17. A rare scalloped Colonial, two-color, punched trim. Scalloped Colonials are very rare.

18. Another fine example: two-color, engine turning and punched design.

19. An engine-turned center with beautifully pierced and engraved border on a two-color button.

20. Pierced with a blued steel center.

21. Faceted blue glass center set in a depression in the metal.

22. Pierced, punched design, silver plated.

23. A rare rimmed Colonial.

24. A punched and engraved basket design.

25. An attractive punched oval design with a raised plain border which has been colored with a blue enamel paint. A cross has been punched between each oval.

26. Opaline glass trim. Punched design.

27. Oval Colonials are rare; this one has a punched design.

28. Engine-turned center with a border of fancy-cut brilliants set in a deep recess.

5

PLATE 6

Fancy Colonials

1.   Sulphide of Neptune made in same manner as button 13 on Plate 5. Blue background. Punched edge.

2.   The flower and leaves which decorate this lovely Colonial have been cut from reinforced silk, decorated with small metal pieces plus tiny seed pearls. Twisted wires are used for stems. All of these items are glued to cobalt blue glass and covered with a high domed glass.

3.   The foliage of this decorative bouquet is painted on cobalt blue glass and the flowers are made of minute seed pearls, all under a high domed glass.

4.   An intaglio-cut female figure of Hope in amethyst glass with a band of two different alternating punched designs.

5.   Painting on ivory of a woman with a spinning wheel, covered with a domed glass. Punched edge.

6.   One of our very earliest discoveries, the only one we ever found with a Wedgwood pinshanked center.

7.   In the eighteenth century the Masonic emblem in France had no G. It is blue enamel. Edge is a punched design.

8.   Surface-painted urn on blue glass. Punched edge.

9.   Sulphide of a warrior, waffle-paper background. This Colonial is silver plated.

10.   This reverse painting of a combination marine and land scene is done in dark sepia shades.

11.   Another reverse painting with background of chipped pearl.

12.   Another sulphide type with a brownish-red background.

13.   Floral decoration done with gold paint on cobalt blue glass. Punched edge.

14.   A handsomely punched wide border with a cobalt blue enamel center, set with a green glass center trimmed with six white pierreries surrounding it.

15.   Surface-painted cobalt blue enamel center adds beauty to this button.

16.   Another Hope painted with gold (églomisé) on blue.

17.   An exquisite Colonial. A seated lady

painted on ivory with a domed glass cover, which has been decorated with a very lacy design edged in blue.

18. This has been called a paperweight type. It does seem to have a set-up of a pressed paper or encliché with glass under and a faceted glass over it. Punched edge.

19. This is another reverse painting, but so different from the other designs characteristic of this type of decoration. It has an églomisé border.

20. A very pretty scallop designed rim with an enamel center painted with gold.

All of these added decorative items are set in a recessed niche; a few have a flange of metal coming up around the glass to hold it securely.

PLATE 7

Enamels of the Eighteenth Century

1 and 3. Enamel-painted designs on cobalt blue enamel. Set in copper with a tin back.

2 and 7. Both of these enamel-trimmed buttons are Colonials. Both are very rare.

4 and 5. Both of these enamel buttons are counter-enameled. Button 4 has surface-painted designs with small pierrerie-like design for the border. Button 5 has gold foil designs laid on the enamel and then fired.

6. Pierrerie-dotted cobalt blue enamel, set in silver with a fine grade of strass.

8. This lovely enamel button is made in the same manner as button 6. It is decorated with a small painted floral spray, and the rest of the top is painted with a conventional gold design.

9 and 10. When one considers the tedious work involved in making these enamel buttons with the very fine, tiny, hard-to-handle foils, which must be laid on by hand and placed so exactly in position, one must appreciate anew the craftsmanship of these artists. The center shows a bird or insect on white enamel, surrounded by white pierreries and blue enamel, with the gold foil pieces as border decoration. These are set in brass with tin backs.

11. Cupid on lion; a grisaille painting done with enamel as base material. Set in copper with tin back.

12. Again, a dark blue enamel with decoration of turquoise blue pierreries, which were placed on gold foil discs and then fired onto the enamel base. Set in metal with brass back.

13 and 14. I have another of these buttons which is broken, and I am astounded by the thinness of the enamel. It seems impossible that it could have been decorated and then fired again. Set in copper with copper back.

15. I am sure this is enameled on gold, as the back is so beautiful and bright. It was presented in a half-round box, with two sizes in the box. Green leaflike foil pieces alternate with red-dotted gold flower heads on black enamel to form a border. The rim is of white pierreries. The center decoration is conventional, with a red dot in the middle of a white design bordered with gold paillons.

16 and 20   These two enamel buttons are set in brass with tin backs. The top one has an opaline glass center and a border of alternating green and white pierreries. The lower one, button 20, has a border of gold foil stars on white enamel, with a conventional center design painted on dark blue enamel.

17, 18, 22, 23.   These four finely executed buttons are among my favorites. They are cut-out, gold silhouettes on dark blue enamel, each one representing a fable. Tiny pieces of foil form an inner border. A white outer border sets off the whole picture. These are counter-enameled.

19.   We might call this an end-o-day decoration. It is enamel set in metal with a tin back.

21.   Another button set as buttons 6 and 8 are.

24.   Cobalt blue enamel with strass center and rim, set in silver gilt.

25.   This button is cracked, granted, but it is so very rare that I have no intention of discarding it. The hunting scene of a man and his dog is set in silver.

26.   The larger circles on this button are flat-backed glass held in position from beneath by a waxlike substance and from the top by brass rings. Again, pierreries are used for decoration. Set in copper with a tin back.

PLATE 8

Eighteenth Century Wedgwoods

Here is an array of Wedgwood jasperware cameos set in a variety of materials.

1, 3, 4, 7. These four from one set are framed in copper.

2. The top center button is pearl with large steels as a border. The cameo was, no doubt, designed by Voyez, an artisan who worked for Josiah Wedgwood for a time.

5, 6, 8, 10. Another four from a set, set on pearl and held in place with a narrow metal ring.

9. The button in the middle is set in a pearl button with a jasper cameo center held in place by a copper ring, and decorated with oblong faceted steels. The twelve buttons of this set were purchased in England, and were framed in two lovely white, oblong frames.

11, 14, 15, 18. Four more which are set in steel, held in place by large faceted steel pins.

12. Another pearl which has a larger cameo with a wider copper ring, held in place with closely-set, faceted steels leaving a narrow border of pearl.

13, 16, 17, 20. This set of four is held with smaller faceted steel pins. Probably these two last sets of four were both made by Matthew Boulton, who was associated with Josiah Wedgwood.

19. The bottom center cameo is set in pearl, which has a copper collet decorated with faceted steels.

These designs were authenticated as being used by Josiah Wedgwood in the eighteenth century by the modern Wedgwood firm in New York. A few are backmarked.

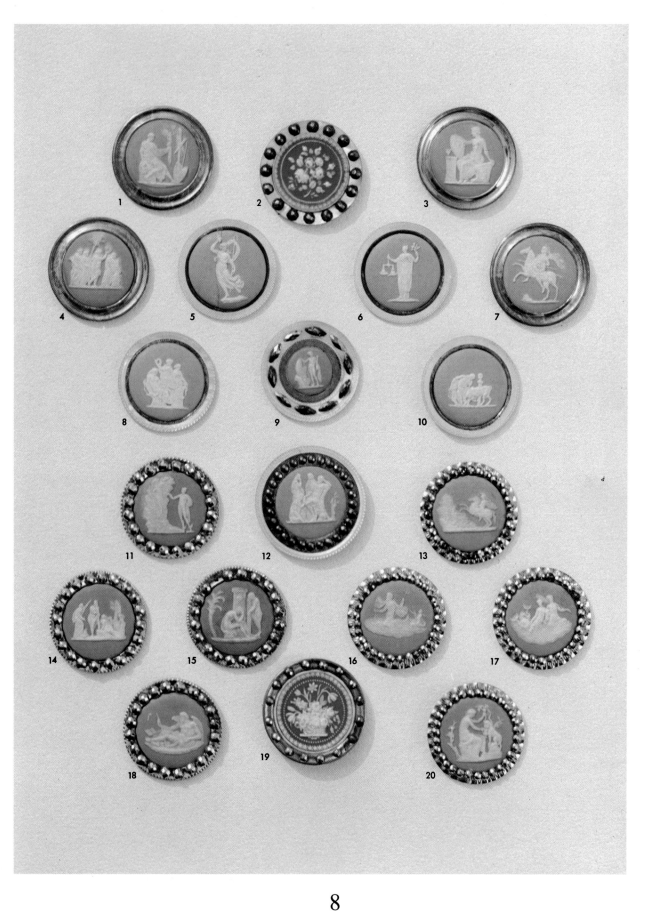

PLATE 9

Eighteenth Century Designs Under Glass

4, 6, 9, 11, 16. These buttons may be as early as 1720, a French authority on antiquities pointed out to me.

5. A very beautiful decoration under glass. A paste (or brilliant) pinshank.

12 and 13. Glass with cut decoration over colored foil.

14 and 23. Reverse paintings with foil decorations added.

15. A painted paper design, colorful and pretty.

17. Small metal squares and stars make an attractive design.

18. Here small pressed paper bits are used in a very effective design.

19. Reverse painting with gold foil in the églomisé technique.

20. A fancy button; red foil placed under glass. A paste and metal pinshank.

All the others on this plate represent different treatments of foil. All are under glass except buttons 12 and 13. All are set in metal and have tin backs except buttons 7, 13 and 20.

PLATE 10

Eighteenth Century Buildings and Scenes

Systematic excavations were begun in 1738 of the city of Herculaneum, which had been destroyed in A.D. 79 by the eruption of Mt. Vesuvius. The many objects discovered in perfect condition inspired artists and builders to use ruins, statues and other art objects in their respective fields. Button-makers shared this enthusiasm, for many sets of buttons have been found showing columns, statues and ruins. Some are pictured on this plate. Exact copies of buildings in France were also a popular subject for buttons.

1. Polychrome scene on parchment with an ivory back.

2 and 4. Soft paste porcelain painted in sepia shades.

3. Scenes are rare on Colonials; this one is copper.

5. Reverse painting with a paper background, set under glass.

6 and 10. Lovely reverse paintings with silver foil placed back of the windows to give it a realistic effect. A background is painted on mica to give a three-dimensional appearance. Set in copper.

7 and 9. These scenes painted on paper show rural activities. Set in brass under glass.

8. This button brings pleasant memories to mind. My husband and I were invited to tea at M. and Mme. Destins' home in a suburb of Paris. They had heard that we were looking for buttons. Their home was furnished with lovely Louis XIV and XV furniture, with eighteenth century pictures on their walls and toile of the same period hanging at their windows. The button pictured was one of a set, and we became the proud owners of the set as well as a few nineteenth century buttons. They are fixé, framed with a steel band and set in a copper rim.

11, 12, 14, 15. Charming polychrome scenes painted on paper, set in gilt; the back comes up on the side around beveled glass.

13. On my first trip to Paris, this button and its mate were found in a small wooden frame designed for them. Both were signed by the artist who drew them with what appears to be ink. They are under glass, with a copper liner and a rim of faceted steels fastened to a white metal back with four metal pins.

16 and 20.　　Paintings on ivory, under glass, with copper collets and tin backs.

17 and 19.　　Printed on parchment, under glass, set in copper with tin backs.

18.　　A very nice fixé scene set in silver with lovely paste border.

21.　　*Faux bois,* or "false wood," the French call this. Painted on ivory. Brass rim and back.

22 and 24.　　These could be Sèvres, as many potters imitated Wedgwood, but the workmanship cannot compare to Wedgwood. These are framed with a sawtoothed band of steel all within a copper collet. Copper back.

23.　　A very colorful scene painted on paper. Copper rim and back.

25.　　Hair was the medium used to paint this scene: a single hair used for lines and hair mashed with mortar and pestle for the massed parts. Copper collet.

26.　　An engraved pearl pigmented to bring out the design, set with a band of steel inside a brass collet.

27.　　Yellow and blue stripes frame this grisaille scene painted on ivory. Copper back.

28 and 33.　　Farm scenes done in the grisaille manner with a blue border around the eight sides.

29.　　A chateau painted on ivory. The rim is copper.

30.　　This lovely scene is painted on pearl with a reverse-painted border in white and gold.

31.　　Découpage, late eighteenth century or early nineteenth century, set in copper, the back coming up around the glass to form the collet.

32 and 34.　　Both of these scenes are reverse decorations; button 32 is a water color, and button 34 an ink. Both have mica backgrounds.

35.　　A three-dimensional effect was achieved here by painting trees and figures on the reverse side of the glass, with a printed, hand-finished-with-color picture on paper behind.

PLATE 11

Eighteenth Century Pearls

These eighteenth century mother-of-pearl buttons, worn on the beautiful velvet and silk coats of the gentlemen of the period, must have made a ballroom a glistening, glistering place of beauty as the candlelight from the chandeliers reflected from the many mirror-trimmed decorations on the buttons. These decorations were varied in shape and color, some clear, some translucent, some opaque, held in place with a waxlike substance. Steel, blued-steel, faceted and plain steel pins, enamel and colored foil were also used. Many were made up of four and five layers of different materials kept in place by a steel or brilliant pinshank, like button 27, which is made up of a brass disc, then a sawtoothed piece of steel, a pearl and then the pinshank of strass.

3. This one has velvet in back of the large jeweled center.

21. A mother-of-pearl button with a jeweled pinshank, brilliantly decorated with opaline glass cabochons, mirrored glass arrowheads, and blue glass pierreries. During the eighteenth century, glass was widely used to simulate precious stones and many of the most beautiful buttons of this period are of this type.

31 and 33. Beautifully engraved pearl with silver applied by the silver-resist process.

PLATE 12

Eighteenth Century Insects and Others

1 and 5. Semi-precious stones have been used to form the bodies and wings of these insects; the stones were ground to such thinness that the body lines on the rock crystal base show through. Set in silver. Supposed to have been made in Ireland in 1794.

2, 7, 12, 17. Buffon was the artist–naturalist supposed to have painted this set of buttons on the reverse side of the glass. They have mica backgrounds. Set in copper.

3, 8, 13, 18. These insects painted on ivory were acquired at the same time as the Buffon buttons and from the same seller, but he did not attribute these ivory ones to Buffon. They are under glass, set in copper.

4, 9, 14, 19. These four reverse-painted insects have a wide border painted on background paper. They, with others, were still on the original sales paper, not a cardboard in this instance. Set in copper.

6. Woven straw, set in brass collet, under glass.

10. This woven hair, under glass and in a copper rim, was very likely a mourning button. Copper collet.

11 and 15. Drawings on paper of containers, with a dolphin design on each one. We were told that these buttons should be in a museum in France because they had been made for the Dauphin, as he alone used a dolphin for his emblem. We were also told by the same informant that the stylized fleur-de-lis on the border or rim was used by Royalty exclusively during certain periods of French history. The rim is silvered copper.

16. This is from a set of sporting buttons which were in very bad condition. I opened and repaired those which I found repairable. These are called *habitat*, as the trees and earth effects are from natural plants. The animals are of a waxlike substance, all affixed to a mica background. Set in brass under domed glass.

20. This wolf, painted in reverse, is one of a set featuring wild animals. Each had a painted tin background and was set in a copper rim.

21. Another habitat made in same manner

as button 16. Real feathers were used for the bird's wings. Set in copper.

22. Pictorial Colonials are rare. This one of a shepherdess and her sheep is hand decorated with a punch and engraved lines.

23. This is an example of the reverse painting of the early eighteenth century, about 1720. It is cracked, but still essential to the collection until I find a perfect one. Set in copper.

24. A donkey of molded wax on a painted tin background.

25. Mosaic bird set in copper.

26. A charming domestic scene painted on paper and under a heavy, faceted glass set in brass, which comes from the back to form the collet.

27 and 29. A rebus is a kind of riddle or puzzle; and rebus buttons contain words, syllables and pictures, which combined sound like other words or phrases. Like Valentines, rebuses deal chiefly with love and its uncertainties. Here rebus sentiments were painted on opaline glass with a circle of flowers near the brass rim. Copper backs.

28. An opaline glass button painted with roses; it has a blue glass pinshank.

30. *Bleu-de-roi* glass over foil, decorated with a silver escutcheon. Set in copper.

31. Pearl trim on a three-color Colonial with a repoussé design and hand-chased edge.

32. A rebus on metal embedded in opaline glass, a pansy (for thoughts) with the French words *a moi* ("of me"). "Think of me."

33. A molded *putto* sitting on a plinth with a blue paper background. Very likely wax or dough.

34. A silver-rimmed pearl disc, surrounded with green cabochon glass jewels, decorates this agate button.

35. This brass Colonial has a chased border and is divided into four equal sections on which a fancy, odd piece of pearl is held in place with faceted steels; a larger faceted steel is set in the center.

PLATE 13

Eighteenth Century Assorted

All of these buttons are set in metal and under glass except the Wedgwoods.

1 and 3. M. Montgolfier's invention of the balloon in the eighteenth century inspired artisans of all crafts to use balloons in their work. Some artists had an exaggerated idea of their utility, as this set, all different, showed. These are reverse drawings in copper rims.

2. This beautiful love token is made on glass with embossed metal or paper trimmed with marcasites and silver pierreries. The border is *bleu-de-roi* foil, under glass and decorated with twisted metal wires and marcasites.

4. Grisaille painting on ivory of a classical subject with a blue background. Copper back.

5. Another sulphide. I wish I could take this button apart to examine it, as the subject matter has depth rather than a filled crystal engraving like the Spanish setter, on Plate 14, button 12. It is set in steel with a copper band, trimmed with faceted steels, holding it in place.

6. An ivory painting in pastel colors of a seated lady.

7 and 8. Painted mythological figures on ivory on a light-blue background, with a white ring decorated with gold and an outer ring of black decorated with garlands of flowers.

9 and 11. Reverse paintings with mica backgrounds.

10. A mourning design of Wedgwood set in fluted steel with a copper rim holding it in place.

12 and 13. Charming paintings of young people in pastoral setting. These are on paper.

14 and 16. Grisaille painting of mythological subjects on ivory with a background of black and an orange border. These were painted by Jean-Jacques Hauer. My husband bought them from the painter's heirs, and we have the authentication. A painting of Charlotte Corday by Hauer hangs in Versailles.

15. A solid ring of faceted steels on copper holds a lovely Wedgwood cameo in place on this pearl button.

17 and 18. Polychrome paintings on ivory of classical subjects.

19 and 21. Polychrome paintings of Moroccans on ivory, framed in a gold-lined oval on a black field.

20 and 25. Two Wedgwood cameos set in heavy steel.

22 and 23. The technique of these carved, or cut-out ivory buttons, is described by Alfred Maskell in his book on ivories: "The method employed was to glue thin sheets of ivory upon wood and with fine gravers and infinite patience the work proceeded, these tiny figures and foliage—the leaves of which a breath would almost suffice to break—these garlands and festoons and open-work were achieved." The background of wine-colored foil brings out the beauty and artistry of the carving. As you can see, the center design is anchored to an outer rim of the ivory disc by foliage or a grassy ground or a garland.

24 and 26. Wax has been used as the art medium for these buttons. It appears that the wax has been applied with a tiny spatula on a fine ribbed silk. I have never seen any others like these buttons.

27 and 28. No doubt these are Wedgwood cameos of Greek or Roman personnages. The backs are wood with four holes in the center through which catgut was drawn in a cross pattern. When sewn to a garment the thread was passed under the crossed catgut. I've seen these strung in a square also; a heavy string or cord was sometimes used.

PLATE 14

Eighteenth Century Assorted

1. This *trompe l'oeil* design is painted on paper. Set in metal.

2. A mourning piece made of tiny seed pearls and embossed paper on *bleu-de-roi* glass. Set in metal; under glass. The back is a thin, silvered brass with several rows of rayed, wavy lines extending from the shank.

3. Grisaille painting of a figure and a small animal in a black ground, framed in a gold ring (églomisé) with an outer border of white. Under glass; set in metal.

4. Needlework, using colored foil to make this pot-of-flowers design. Darned back.

5. Lovers painted on enamel decorate this button set in silver.

6. A bird embroidered with gold thread on a gold cloth with a gold-thread embroidered edge. Bead eyes.

7. Glass protects this painting on pearl of a bouquet.

8. A portrait of M. de Lafayette painted on paper. Copper rim.

9. Another needlework button using white and blue pierreries, sequins and brass rosettes to hold the blue pierreries on white satin. Gold beads are used to finish the outer edge.

10. A metal button of the Empire period.

11. This tassel and garland are a combination of sequins and embroidery with gold thread on gold foil. Same edge as button 21.

12. See description of the Stubbs setter button in the Introduction, page xii, and a comparison with button 5 on Plate 13.

13. Cut-out ivory. Refer to Plate 13, buttons 22 and 23.

14. Beautifully executed mosaic butterfly set in metal, the back coming up around the mosaic to form a collet.

15. A circlet of Wedgwood set in steel.

16. Inlay of gold and copper paillons in real tortoiseshell with a carved pearl piece in the center over gold foil.

17 and 18. "Renos and St. Aubin." These buttons are from a set telling a story about chimney sweeps. Sweeps must have been a popular subject, because a number of such sets have been

unearthed, some on paper, some on ivory. Set in brass under glass. These are painted on ivory.

19. Colored embossed starlike foil pieces have been placed on a base of loosely woven gold thread, which is over silver foil. This has a thick glass cover, cut around the edge with a half-round design; all set in silver gilt.

20. Reticulated Royal Copenhagen, signed.

21. A colorful needlework button with handmade lace in the center surrounded by embroidered sequins and medallions of looped thread, in the center of which is a jewel. This work is done on red foil. Same edge as button 11.

22. A marine scene painted on mica with realistic wax soldiers in a boat. Set in copper rim under glass.

23. A fine example of passementerie using gold thread, decorations under glass and paste jewels. Large ones are rare.

24. An unusual basket of flowers, fashioned from seed pearls, twisted wires and pressed or molded paper, seems to be suspended within a glass ball. The ball is in two equal parts which are held together with a brass collet.

14

PLATE **15**

Eighteenth Century Assorted

1, 4, 5, 7. Delicately painted designs on the reverse side of the glass. Mica background.

2, 3, 8, 9, 21, 22, 26, 27. This set of buttons depicts occupations—even to a wet nurse. Polychrome paintings on paper.

6, 11, 18, 24. Sulphides, three with blue and one with black background.

10, 12, 17, 19. Beautifully executed grisaille paintings on ivory of mythological subjects. They are under glass, set in metal and have pearl backs.

13, 14, 15, 16. Set of dancing girls.

20, 23, 25, 28. The detail in this set of buttons is very fine; they are painted on parchment.

All these buttons are set in metal under glass.

15

PLATE 16

Eighteenth Century Assorted

1 and 3. These paintings on ivory are copied from the larger paintings done by the eighteenth-century French painter, Boucher. They are done in lovely pastel shades. Set in metal, under glass, with brass backs. The first is called "The Fisherman." It is very like the original, but was painted in reverse. Button 3, "Rustic Love," or "Love in the Country," is a very good copy. Other buttons in the set showed "The Love Message," "Garden Scene," "The German Dance," etc.

2. A very rare brass button because of its size and shape as well as for its subject matter. The balloon is of repoussé silver, attached by a pin through the body of the button and bent over on the back. The border and garlands are hand chased. The balloon, first perfected in flight by the Montgolfier brothers during the last decades of the eighteenth century, became a favorite decorative motif, but it was rarely found on Colonial buttons.

4 and 7. Classical figures painted in gold-trimmed grisaille technique on ivory; the black backgrounds are sprinkled with gold and pearl flecks.

5 and 6. Two of the Muses printed on silk with églomisé borders on the reverse side of the glass.

8 and 9. Two other Muses printed on silk and hand-tinted in color. The border is painted on the reverse side of the glass. All four Muses are set in metal and are under glass with brass backs.

10, 11, 12, 13. Carved conch shell is the medium for these heads of four Caesars, all set in a border of fine strass.

14, 15, 16. Mythological subjects painted on silk in grisaille. Under glass and set in metal.

17, 18, 19, 20. A group of copper Colonials, the center of which is depressed to take the hand-tinted printed silk made to fit it.

21 and 23. Two more Wedgwood cameos set like the others we have seen.

22. This rebus is made up of two ovals of ivory which have been painted and placed under glass. The glass has been decorated in the églomisé manner on the reverse side to frame the two ivory pieces. Set in copper.

24 and 25. Grisaille paintings on paper with blue backgrounds. Set in metal under glass with copper backs.

26 and 28. Grisaille heads on ivory, under glass, set in copper.

27. Another rebus, this one is porcelain with a self-shank. It is a larger than usual button and dish-shaped. Hand painted.

16

PLATE 17

Eighteenth and Nineteenth Century Variety

1, 2, 3, 5. These beautiful buttons are later than the eighteenth century period. Miniatures on ivory surrounded with paste jewels.

4. A large eighteenth century jeweled button with a strass center surrounded with opaline pierreries, against a circle of beautiful deep-purple amethyst cabochon sparklers. All of this within a strass border and set in silver.

6. A lovely bouquet of roses painted on porcelain. A circle of brass lies within the copper rim.

7, 8, 10. Mythological figures painted on ivory in the grisaille manner. Copper rims and copper back.

9 and 11. Two Colonials of rare design.

12, 13, 17, 18. Pastoral scenes painted in soft shades on paper. Copper collets.

14. This fine button has a pastel painting on ivory, framed with two types of decorations: one a tiny chain; the other tiny embossed silver flowerettes, with gold garlands above and below. All of this is on red foil. Set in brass.

15. From the strass center of this under-glass decorated button radiate ten starlike prongs of foil, each tipped with three tiny paillons; between each pair of rays is a gold star. The back of the glass is painted gray. The collet is rather wide and fluted.

16. Another cut-out ivory on a red foil background.

19 and 21. Two more from the occupations set also shown on Plate 15.

20, 22, 23, 24. Heads of ladies printed on paper and finished by hand with color. High-domed glass set in brass.

PLATE **18**

Eighteenth and Nineteenth Century Deluxe Buttons

1 and 5. These under-glass examples are painted on pearl. Button 1 has a conical glass top, and button 5 has a faceted glass top; both are set in metal.

2. This is a black-glass molded head of Queen Victoria. It has indentations so that heavy thread can be laced in a design. The threads are gathered together on the back and then sewn together. To sew the button to a garment, it was necessary to sew under these threads.

3. A frosted and faceted black-glass paperweight button.

4. Made in the same manner as button 2, but with narrow ribbon. These groved and laced buttons are very rare.

6. Lowestoft. The colorings and base material of this eighteenth century porcelain, set in metal with a tin back, certainly qualify as Lowestoft. The only one I've ever seen.

7. "Little Red Riding Hood" transfer on self-shanked porcelain.

8. Encliché basket set in metal in an ivory button. Eighteenth or early nineteenth century.

9. Carved conch shell scene set in pronged metal with faceted steel border.

10. Mother-of-pearl with gold and silver leaf design; blue pierreries dot the border.

11, 15, 16, 20. Mrs. Lillian Albert and I worked on acquiring a card of these buttons, which we both felt were transitional; that is, they carry some eighteenth century features over into the early nineteenth century, but date from before the Golden Age buttons of the period 1830 to 1850. Needlework, stamped-out metal trim, pierced and carved pearl, or sequins and paste are all used on this type of button. Some have metal backs; others are darned. Neither Mrs. Albert nor I ever finished a "thirty"-card.

12 and 14. Two of a set of fable buttons. Mother-of-pearl, made in the same manner as buttons 31 and 33 on Plate 11. Eighteenth century.

13. Carved conch shell head. A very fancy cut-out border studded with faceted steels.

17. Star-cut glass over silver foil on a flat brass back.

18. Another example of eighteenth century

fine handwork. Floral design made with delicate gold wires, and a border of wire rings with steel shavings in each ring. Red and green paint used for flowers and leaves. All on opaline glass.

19. An unusually large-cut overlay kaleidoscope.

21. Very nicely carved conch shell cameo set in prongs, with a paste border. All in metal.

22. Marvelously executed castle scene on porcelain, set in sterling.

23. "Maine." A commemorative mother-of-pearl button, partly engraved and pigmented, and carved, with *Maine* on a banner across the water lines.

24. Another lovely porcelain of a young woman. Set in metal with a paste rim.

25. An attractive, irregularly oval, jeweled button.

26 and 27. Needlework of the eighteenth century. This size was used on "gilets," or vests. Gold foil on button 26, and silver foil on button 27, embroidered with gold threads.

28. Agate with gold rim and pinshank. Colonial.

29. Colored gold enhances the repoussé flowers and leaves of this design. A very pretty border. Hallmarked with two stars, fleur-de-lis, crown and the word *double.*

30. Very complex. Radiating from the faceted steel pinshank are six fancy pieces of cut flat steel, which are "pinned" to the outer border of partially-blued steel. Carved, fanlike mother-of-pearl pieces form the center of the button. Eighteenth century.

31. Counter-enameled floral enamel with backmark.

32. Eighteenth century large gold-thread needlework button with ovate mirror glass decoration and large paste center.

33. A beautiful eighteenth century jeweled button set in metal with open back.

34. Carved mother-of-pearl deer, set in a flat-backed piece of brass, with prongs holding the pearl in place.

PLATE **19**

Assorted Buttons

1. Encliché basket set under glass, with a border of red and gold foil paillons. All in metal with tin back. Eighteenth century.

2. Enamel. Shepherdess design surrounded by red glass with five strass set on the glass, the whole surrounded with fine strass.

3. A fine coaching scene on pinna shell. This one is extra large. Engraved and pigmented with a whitish material.

4. A fine scenic mosaic made in red glass and set in gold.

5. Miniature of a pretty girl set in a fancy scalloped frame of what appears to be smoked paste.

6. Octagonal silver depicting a monk and a farmer perhaps. This button could be as early as the first half of the seventeenth century.

7. Two-color metal makes up this pierced metal button showing a basket of flowers.

8. Basse-taille enamel on sterling, with a sterling basket trimmed with marcasite and held to the back by turned-over pins.

9 and 13. These small Wedgwood buttons are self-shanked and marked on the back.

10 and 12. These are reverse paintings on glass, the tops being concave. Set in prongs and trimmed with a border of paste.

11. This is a marked Lalique. It is beautiful frosted glass, molded to show a coiled cobra. Set in metal.

14. Amethyst quartz carved with two birds makes this a very desirable button for a collection. Self-shank.

15. Rose quartz with a gold pinshank.

16. Lacy iridescent glass with a paste pinshank. The appearance of amber jewels was achieved by painting the back of the button in those places where the front was molded and faceted like jewels.

17. A silverlike poppy made of pearls set on amber glass over a lovely design in relief. All set in white metal.

18. Opaque glass with design of coralline.

19. Conch shell head set in prongs with paste border.

20. Painted porcelain of a dancing man

playing a lute. Set in sterling.

21, 35, 46. These three buttons are intaglio molded glass designs filled with pigment. A caribou, lily of the valley, and forget-me-nots, with pearl backgrounds. All are set in metal.

22. Lamb mosaic in black glass. Gold setting.

23. A Kate Greenaway design cut out of metal and attached to wood which has a raised edge, making a nice rim.

24. This is tooled leather set in metal with a shieldlike design. Backmarked *Paris, Solidite, 27.*

25 and 26. Mosaic animals made in gold stoneglass and set in sterling.

27. Peacock eye set in prongs with paste border.

28, 29, 30. Three celluloid buttons; one has a lithograph head; the one on the right an escutcheon of Jeanne d'Arc with a steel in each corner of the square button; the extra-large one has an escutcheon of an owl and grain held to base with faceted steels.

31. An under-glass peacock eye with the domed top lined and filled with gold lustre outlining a peacock. Set in metal.

32. There are few solid tortoise buttons: this one has a Florentine inlay center. Faceted steels trim the outer border.

33. Black glass with three gold lustre fish, a symbol of the Trinity.

34. Gold button with woven human hair under four twisted gold wires; there is a small pin head in the center.

36. Horn button molded in a likeness of Abraham Lincoln.

37 and 41. Painted heads on porcelain set in metal with a brilliant border.

38. Pink and white opaque glass set in metal.

39. Paperweight of cranberry glass with a sulphide head.

40. Precision inlay, clear glass in opaque glass. Set in metal.

42. A bee hovering near bachelor-buttons painted on paper and set in clear horn, with a top rim of tortoiseshell. Glass top.

43. Glass painted on the reverse side and set in brass, with surface decoration of faceted steels and brass balls forming a five-point star.

44. A damascene design of birds with a jade border. Set in brass.

45. Pinna shell decorated with a stylized, etched star design and inlaid with eight flat pieces of steel.

47 and 49. A floral and a good-luck design painted on pearl and under glass. Set in brass.

48. A basket of flowers done in petit point. Under glass and set in silver.

50. Cloth-covered high convex mold with a decoration of an enameled holly leaf and four small brilliants for the holly berries.

51. Inlay in solid tortoise. Unusual in that, generally, a thin piece of tortoise was laminated to a horn base.

PLATE 20

Assorted Buttons

1. Porcelain with hand-painted detail added to a decal. Silver-resist collet.

2. Pierced brass with enamel and paste jewels.

3. The tip of a real shell with its bark partially polished away and set in metal.

4. A beautiful reverse-intaglio head in glass. The entire back of the glass painted in metallic paint, set in decorative prongs, and rimmed with paste jewels.

5. Small floral porcelain with backmark *Minton*.

6. Porcelain set in metal: man's figure.

7. Pierced enamel trim applied with cut-steel rivets to pierced and carved smoky pearl.

8. Porcelain set in metal: woman's figure.

9. Realistic porcelain rose like those often found on Dresden figurines.

10. Cartouche-shaped, painted enamel head with champlevé border and rim of tiny paste jewels.

11. Mosaic figure of a dog, inlaid in black glass and set in silver gilt.

12. Mosaic figure of a cat, inlaid in black glass and set in silver gilt.

13. Realistic lacy glass leaf. These are called "lacy glass" in button collecting because their textured surface resembles the so-called lacy effect of Sandwich glass pieces.

14. A counter-enameled (enameled on back as well as front) button with floral basket painted design and a gold foil border near the edge.

15. An 18k. gold button set with lavender glass, a pearl in the center, and trimmed with white enamel. This button could be as early as 1551: Mary, Queen of Scots, reference *Trésorier des Enfants de France*.

16. Cloisonné enamel of wisteria and a butterfly.

17. A monkey's face carved from labradorite and set in gold. A vest button.

18. Hallmarked silver: pastoral scene.

19. Enamel and solid gold. Could be from the same period as button 15.

20. Unusually fine mosaic basket of flowers,

inlaid in terracotta opaque glass, and set in gold.

21. A finely detailed, reverse-intaglio head within a narrow band of leaves and surrounded by a flat border. The head and border are painted on the back of the glass with gold paint, while the area surrounding the head is painted brown and the leaves are painted green. The top surface of the glass has been molded with a raised pattern of eight bees above the flat border on the back. The bees still show evidence of gold luster. The entire button is set in metal.

22. Porcelain with hand-painted bird and foliage.

23. Realistic thistle, trimmed with paste jewels and applied to a pierced metal base of heavy brass. Entire button finished in a silverlike finish.

24. Carved and pierced wood button with triangular pieces of abalone shell inlaid in the border and a carved griffin center motif of smoky pearl.

25. Anchor and oars carved of smoky pearl and secured to the face of a wooden button with cut-steel rivets.

26. Realistic rose of molded and pierced brass, trimmed with enamel and paste jewels.

27. Lithograph head set in dyed vegetable ivory.

28. Wading bird beneath a tree, parti-enameled. Attached, pierced border of alternating paste jewels and dark blue enamel sections.

29. Deeply repoussé brass head with a border of blue pierreries.

30. Very early transfer head on silvered paper, set in a metal rim, and with a thread-back.

31. Realistic enameled flower with a single paste jewel in the center, secured at three points to a shaped metal ring trimmed with paste jewels.

32. A child's figure painted on white sheet overlay, cut away at the border to show the nearly-clear glass under layer, and set in a border of brass with shaped prongs. Shank secured to a bar across the back of the button.

33. Early, floral painted porcelain. Hollow and with three-hole, sew-through requiring a curved needle for sewing to garment. No back-mark.

34. Porcelain Cupid in bisque with a raised and gilded border. Outer edge and back of button are glazed. Self-shank. Sèvres mark.

35. Solid gold button of pierced and molded leaves.

36. Wedgwood, with steel pinshank and a flat metal back plate.

37. Small scalloped button of gold and silver set with rubies and rose-cut diamonds.

38. Opaque white glass, painted with a rose, and trimmed with coralline.

39. Wood marquetry design of lilies of the valley.

40. Solid gold button with a French back-mark indicating the year 1754.

41. Pierced brass and amber paste jewels secured to the face of a horn button. Metal of back does not fully cover the back of this button. Shank embedded in the exposed horn.

42. Sulphide-like liberty head and stars impressed in the back of the glass with a glued-on metal back plate and shank. A rare kaleidoscope.

43. A frog carved from red coral and with a self-shank.

44. A flat watch crystal of glass, painted on the back in black and gold to outline a clear glass figure. Thin bits of abalone, attached to the flat metal shank plate, show through the clear glass area to add color and interest to the button.

45. A beautifully carved, mother-of-pearl escutcheon of a bee and a flower is secured to the engraved wood button by means of two cut-steel rivets.

46. The Eiffel Tower carved from smoky pearl and secured to the white, engraved mother-of-pearl button by two cut-steel rivets.

47. Oriental figure on yellow and white metals inlaid in nearly transparent horn.

48. Finely painted enamel head with delicately cut foil trim.

49. Hand-painted on paper, set in gold.

50. Smoky pearl set in metal, under a finely detailed and cut-out design. The French call buttons of this construction *pom-poms*.

51. Finely painted enamel head with delicately cut foil trim. Very similar to button 48.

52. A whimsical little button of a bird sitting on a telephone wire. Highly three-dimensional with the telephone pole protruding far to the foreground. Brass.

53. A finely-carved head of conch shell, set in metal, with an enameled border secured to the back by means of four cut-steel rivets.

54. A brass escutcheon, in the form of the British coat of arms, affixed to a wooden button by means of the shank.

PLATE 21

Assorted Buttons

1.   Miniature portrait painting on ivory, set in metal under glass, and rimmed with fine paste jewels.

2.   Beautifully carved man's head in lava, in very high relief, and set in gold.

3.   A molded-in-relief porcelain head set in metal. The head itself is unglazed but painted; it must have been fired after decoration. The rest of the top is glazed.

4, 18, 20.   Metal buttons with thin wafer of pearl affixed to form part of the design; over-painted with background color and the balance of the design.

5.   Dark smoky pearl, engraved with a design of flowers and leaves. Trimmed with a lovely, molded brass, art nouveau design of iris secured to the pearl by means of three cut-steel rivets. The blooms are painted lavender.

6.   Smoky pearl makes a beautiful background for this lovely swan and iris of brass with a silver wash.

7.   Bird and leaves of silver set with paste jewels. Entire area surrounding the design is enameled in red.

8.   Bird in a tree painted on ivory. Set in silver and under glass.

9.   Insect set in metal. Design achieved in essentially the same manner as watch crystal described in Plate 20, button 44.

10.   Miniature portrait painted on ivory, set in metal under glass and rimmed with paste jewels.

11.   Highly three-dimensional carved pearl scene set in metal. In addition to the carving, the pearl is etched with gold paint laid in.

12.   Bird and nest carved in smoky pearl and secured to a smoky pearl base by means of four cut-steel rivets. Three of the steels comprise the eggs in the nest. The bird has a red glass eye.

13.   An etched design on mother-of-pearl, pigmented in gold, with an applied border of carved smoky pearl leaves and flowers secured to the button by three cut-steel rivets.

14.   Scalloped enamel button trimmed with delicately cut gold foil. Counter-enameled; see Plate 20, button 14.

15. Embroidered lawn of the period from 1780 to 1810.

16. Head carved in shaded pearl. The front surface only has a border of brass set with cut-steel rivets.

17. Cameo head framed with delicately engraved metal; the intricate border design is accented with black enamel paint.

19. A square, white opaque glass button, with cut-off corners. A molded design of an Oriental figure is set in a border of flowers and insect. Over-washed with brown paint. Worn places accent the design and highlight the subject.

21. Beautiful, realistic poppy decorated in polychrome enamel.

22. Lovely rose-glazed porcelain button with a raised, molded border design. The design and rim are gilded.

23. Scene carved in shaded pearl, set in metal, and with a paste jeweled rim.

24. Extra-large, engraved and pigmented white jade button with a self-shank requiring a curved needle to sew it on material.

25. "Pegasus." Reverse intaglio in glass with paint laid into the design and on back of glass. Set in metal.

26. Fan with cord and tassel carved in beautifully shaded smoky pearl.

27. An early Wedgwood, backmarked and self-shanked.

28. Realistically shaped enamel butterfly, champlevé method.

29. Belgian lion embroidered in gold and red on black silk. Late eighteenth or early nineteenth century.

30. Painted figures of a boy and a woman on bone.

31. Encliché metal design, decorated in enamel, and set in metal under glass.

32. Realistic enamel pansy trimmed with two paste jewels.

33. Brass flower and leaves set with paste jewels. Area surrounding the design is enameled, shading from deep rose to white.

34. Eighteenth century button of scalloped steel, with half of each scallop blued. Carved mother-of-pearl layer; notched edges show a thin sheet of copper set in recessed center of steel button. Pearl and copper sheets both secured to steel by means of a paste jeweled, silver pin-shank.

35. Two-part pearl button. A pierced carving of trees in smoky pearl is secured to the highly iridescent base of abalone by means of ten cut-steel rivets.

36. A large, squarish button of silvered brass set with shaped amethyst glass stones and paste jewels.

PLATE 22

Assorted Buttons

1. A wild rose on two colors of metal trimmed with brilliants. Art nouveau design.

2. A molded glass peacock with under-glass coloring set in a brass back and collet.

3. Pearl centered plique-à-jour of two colors. Held to the light, plique-à-jour is translucent.

4. Another under-glass design with a pressed glass top. Center and one of the bands are finished with gold lustre.

5. This design was taken from the "Triumphal Entry of Alexander the Great into Babylon" by Thorwaldson. It is a reverse intaglio filled with a sulphidelike substance. Set in brass.

6. A carved and painted floral design on ivory. Art nouveau design.

7. A transfer design of water birds and plants on vegetable ivory. Vegetable ivory, from the corozo or tagua nut, rarely yields buttons of this size.

8. Opal-like center in a cut-out horn design of leaves. Art nouveau design.

9, 11, 13. Three very fine and varied examples of decorated metal buttons.

10. Many parts make up this floral design. The individual flowers are painted with a light enamel; each one is attached separately to wires of different lengths out of the center of the back. The shank is attached to a bar reaching across the back.

12. This button is made of blue beads strung to a wire base with steel beads.

14. A colorful transfer pattern on pearl.

15. Opaque glass with a strawberry design.

16. Ovate crystal with escutcheon of paste; brilliant-trimmed metal lizard.

17. A flower of faceted steels on a pretty brass button. Art nouveau design.

18. Floral transfer on pearl. This button is delicate and easily scratched.

19. Metal basket trimmed with marcasites on smoky pearl.

20. Inlay of a bird and garland in solid tortoiseshell.

21. Three moths with their heads to the center form this lovely horn button. They are

delicately tinted with grey and have a greenish paste center.

22.   A sew-through watch crystal. The floral decoration is outlined in gold on the reverse side and placed over a base of pearl chips, which have been cemented on pitch; all are held to a flat back with sealing wax.

23.   A two-color metal, art nouveau button.

24.   Another marcasite-trimmed button of two colors of metal.

25.   A bat with spread wings near the bottom of this button and a small one flying above add to the interest of this lady's head, set under glass. The button honors the operetta, *Die Fleder-maus.*

26.   An interestingly shaped pearl deco-rated with gold foil and a small attached carved rose.

27.   The description of button 22 applies to this one, too, except that glass and pearl parts are set in metal.

28.   Straw set in metal with a small floral enamel center.

29 *and* 33.   Two different roses made of vegetable ivory (tagua nut) and wood. They are held in place by screws from the back of the button.

30.   Art nouveau design of a girl's head and flowers. Two-color metal.

31.   Solid gold.

32.   A lovely iris on a lacy ground. Art nouveau design.

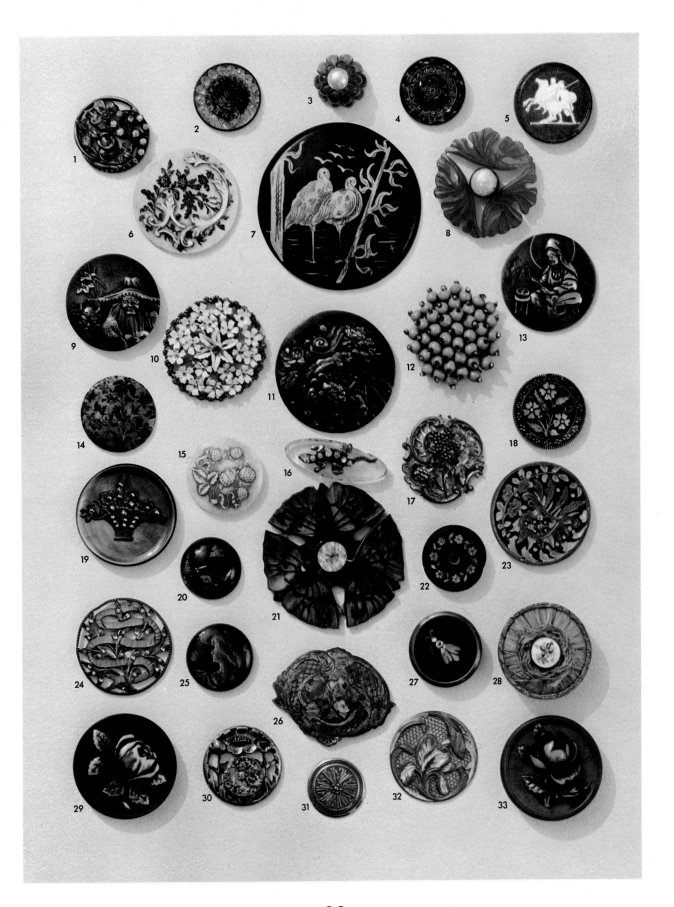

PLATE 23

Porcelains and Enamels

1. Surface painted enamel on transparent enamel design of a daffodil.

2. A fine plique-à-jour enamel set with small brilliants. See Plate 22, button 3.

3. A bow of plique-à-jour enamel set in a solid mass of brilliants, or paste.

4. Gold-painted floral design on enamel. This paint and that on button 1 are discernible to the touch.

5. Beautifully decorated with colored pierreries and gold foil over green basse-taille enamel, with pearl-like pierreries as a border, this enamel piece is set in metal with faceted steels around the edge.

6. A design of faceted steels decorates the open center of this champlevé enamel button which also has a scalloped border of faceted steels.

7. Floral porcelain set in silver gilt. The decoration and basketweave top of this button are very similar to Mennecy porcelain pieces. No backmark.

8. The escutcheon and rim of this porcelain piece make it very attractive. Set in silver gilt.

9. Cloisonné enamel flower set in silver.

10. A painted scene on porcelain.

11. A backmarked Wedgwood button, circa 1890's.

12. The picture shows the lovely front of this cloisonné rose but not the back which is almost as pretty. The back is covered with many ice-blue impressed foils, some of butterflies, under transparent enamel.

13. A realistic enamel pansy face with a blue-glass center.

14. A hollow button, with four holes in back for sewing to garment, such as we have found on buttons having crossed swords. This one has a basketweave top, but it is not like that on buttons 7 and 10.

15. Eighteenth century soft paste with rose decoration.

16. An item made like button 14 but with a smooth top decorated with forget-me-nots. Crossed swords.

17. *Pâté-sur-pâté* (paste-on-paste), with a flying crane design.

18. A signed Minton button.

19. *Pâté-sur-pâté* leaflike design. These are from the latter part of nineteenth century.

20. Wedgwood jasper cameo set in steel with faceted steels in the border. Eighteenth century.

21. Hand-painted wreath of flowers on an eighteenth century porcelain with a jeweled pin-shank.

22 and 24. Gold-bordered floral bouquets on porcelain. Crossed swords. Self-shank.

23. Satsuma ware.

25. Pansy face design of Royal Copenhagen.

26. A very dainty porcelain piece with a raised or embossed painted design. Set in metal.

27, 28, 29. Lovely hand-painted birds on items constructed like button 14.

30. A shepherdess painted on steel-trimmed champlevé enamel.

PLATE 24

Pearl and Shell

1. Hand-carved mother-of-pearl head on a base of abalone shell.

2. Smoky pearl set in metal with enameled and jeweled floral escutcheon and a rim of enamel.

3. A scene carved from shaded pearl, from dark to light, set in metal with paste border held to the shank with four spokes.

4. A two-color metal rose escutcheon on mother-of-pearl set in metal. *T.W.W.* backmarked.

5. This carved mother-of-pearl lily has been decorated with gold paint.

6. Pierced oval sew-through with a metal border the same shape and held to the base with steels.

7. Bouquet of flowers carved from abalone shell.

8. The roses on this concave abalone shell button are carved from mother-of-pearl, tinted pink and placed in recessed holes.

9. A female figure, perhaps a Muse, carved from conch shell. Set in silver.

10. Transfer design of plant life on pearl.

11. A daisy painted on pearl, under glass and set in metal. The shank is very large; no doubt this was a vest button.

12. This water bird standing among aquatic plants, all made of metal, is attached to a faceted-steel rim back. The background is pierced mother-of-pearl.

13. Evidently vest buttons were very popular as they are found in so many different designs and settings. This one is a floral design under glass, set in metal.

14. Small carving of a seated lady and dog. It is square, a sew-through and of smoky pearl.

15. Carved sheaf of wheat with a steel sickle pinned to the smoky pearl.

16. Gold and silver foil were used to make this recessed floral design. The raised rim is studded with blue pierreries.

17. Coachmen wore these large engraved buttons, which were pigmented with a black substance like lamp black.

18. A carved Easter lily held to a wooden button by faceted steels. Button 16 and this one are of mother-of-pearl.

19.   Carved, pierced mother-of-pearl with a lovely metal decoration of iris.

20.   The enamel center in this mother-of-pearl button is laced with gold wire and set in metal.

21.   This chicken head is carved from pearl, shaded from dark to light.

22.   Smoky pearl with a chrysanthemum done in same manner as button 16; decorated with green jewels.

23.   This smoky pearl has an escutcheon of a child and jumping Jack.

24.   Shaded pearl carved from dark to light with a carved rose of pink shell added.

25.   Mother-of-pearl set in metal. A metal laurel wreath studded with steels circles the pearl; a red jewel in the center. Directoire period.

26.   Pierced smoky pearl, rose design with gold paint added for decoration as well as an edge of riveted steels and an inner border of fancy, embossed brass, which frames the pierced design.

27.   Gold lustre trims the fan of shaded pearl, carved from dark to light.

28 and 30.   Floral designs etched on pearl and pigmented with red.

29.   A metal morning-glory escutcheon on smoky pearl. A shanked flat plate is attached to the back of the pearl with metal pins.

31.   An elephant painted in blue.

32.   Pierced shaded pearl.

33.   Red-dyed pearl.

34.   Carved, shaded pearl, of a scene. With an unusual border of paste.

35.   Carved cowry shell scene.

36.   An openwork metal button of an iris, which has a background of abalone shell.

37.   A carved conch scene.

38.   Two parts make up this button; the bottom part is of mother-of-pearl with a bird in a horseshoe carved from smoky pearl and secured to the base with four cut-steels.

39.   A lovely carved iris from cowry shell.

40.   An eagle carved from mother-of-pearl on a smoky pearl base.

41.   Carved, pierced smoky pearl with ring of metal and faceted steels.

42.   Carved smoky pearl held to a white pearl base with faceted steels.

43.   A scene in carved, shaded pearl.

44.   Separately carved anchor on smoky pearl, on which there are gold painted oars.

45.   The base of this button is wood; a thin sheet of smoky pearl tops that with its metal escutcheon of iris trimmed with steels.

46.   Another shaded pearl carved from dark to light of a man walking.

47.   Same as button 46, but with a metal escutcheon of Athene in the center.

48.   Insect carved from one layer to another of abalone.

49.   A heavy piece of shell which has been inlaid with chips of abalone.

50.   Smoky pearl with inlay of a bunch of grapes from abalone shell.

PLATE 25

Assorted Enamels

1 and 5. These are counter-enameled, rolled-edge buttons.

2, 3, 4, 6, 7, 9, 10. Lovely Battersea type of enamel, beautifully made.

8. We were told in France that this type of enamel (with the silver decoration) was made in the early nineteenth century in Switzerland.

11, 13, 22, 33. Pierced metal with parti-enamel; some with paste trim; circa 1900.

12. A marine scene basse-taille inset in silver made in the Orient.

14. The fable of Terces and Annetts is the subject matter of this enamel button.

15. This button and five others (buttons 17, 21, 23, 27, 29) form a circle. They are painted enamel heads with fancy borders.

16. A fairly high-domed cloisonné button said to be of Russian origin, circa 1825.

18. An Oriental-designed dragon, set in metal.

19 and 20. Looking down at button 19 one would think of a plate — the scalloped edge is raised above a flat, recessed center. Foil is used as well as paillons to decorate button 20; the bottom rows on each are of cloisonné enamel.

24. Lovely Limoges enamel head. When you rub your finger across the top of this button you can feel "waves," an indication of its origin. Set in silver.

25. An oval with a full-figured lady. There are several designs. Paste or steels are used as borders on these buttons, which come in blue as well as this wine color.

26. A *putto* on dark blue enamel, set in metal, with a rope border.

28. Paste set in metal surrounds this basse-taille enamel with gold foil paillons, and flowerlike center made up of white and a red pierreries.

30. A slightly concave enamel showing a *putto* holding a bird. Set in metal with paste border.

31. Some say this is Jeanne d'Arc. The figure is on a pale blue enamel. Paris backmark.

32. I've seen only a few enamel buttons similar to this one; they appear to consist of a pressed design with transparent enamel over all, set in metal. They are thin buttons.

34. Lucky is the person who finds such a four-leaf clover as this. Small blue pierreries make up the border.

35. An early paillon-trimmed basse-taille, jeweled enamel set in a lovely silver mounting.

36. This button is almost as high-domed as it is wide. It has a very thin enamel-painted figured design.

37. Four intertwined silver decorative rings enhance the beauty of this foil-trimmed transparent enamel with a coral center.

38. A lovely silver button trimmed with plain as well as flower-painted enamel.

39 through 43. These are all true cloisonnés, fine examples of a rather scarce type of button.

PLATE 26

Ivory

These ivories are painted, carved and pigmented, with one having a transfer design.

4 and 21. Very likely these thick buttons were used on an opera cape. The top one is solid with a screw-in shank, and it is signed. The bottom one is hollowed out and requires a curved needle to sew it to a garment. Both are of floral design.

12. This button with a fruit design is a thread-back, and if you look closely you can see where the stitches are sewn through the holes made in the edge of the ivory and then woven across the back.

13. This has a damascene trim held to the ivory by three pins cut off flush with the ivory.

17. A carving of a lovely Oriental lady. This is set in silver and backmarked *Vantines*. It is signed on the face of the button.

26

PLATE 27

Under Glass

These are a specialty of mine. They are hand-painted on pearl in most instances, set under glass, which is sometimes also painted as well as faceted. The setting is metal.

3 and 13.   These are encliché.

21.   This button is satin, but also comes within the category, "under glass."

22.   A reverse intaglio rose painted with a decorated base.

27

PLATE 28

Metal Picture Buttons

I do not collect picture buttons except certain ones which are especially appealing. Those on this plate are self-explanatory and my favorite metals.

2. Medusa has many snakes for hair.

4. The lower part of the jockey on the fish is wood.

5. The two-color metal boat is another design taken from "The Triumphal Entry of Alexander the Great into Babylon" frieze by Thorwaldson.

6. The wheelbarrow of flowers is white metal on japanned brass.

10 and 12. These two buttons deserve an explanation. They contain portraits of Victoria and Albert, but it's the backs which are interesting. The shank is on a small, square piece of metal which fits precisely in a square in the button and is kept in place by turning the shank while pressing on it after inserting it in the square opening. Back-marked *Bridges Patent.*

20. This head of Athene was my first button, given to me by Hanna Kohn in 1941.

PLATE 29

Jeweled Buttons

Since these buttons are presented in color, the materials from which they are made are, for the most part, self-explanatory.

6 and 15. Both are eighteenth century and set in silver, but they are treated differently in their settings. Button 6 is cut out, while 15 is set solidly with cut opaline petal-like glass and strass.

16. This button is made up of steels as trim over green transparent enamel.

18. A most interesting construction, the lilylike flower being made of faceted steels with a background of fabric. Look closely and you can see where the fabric is worn through.

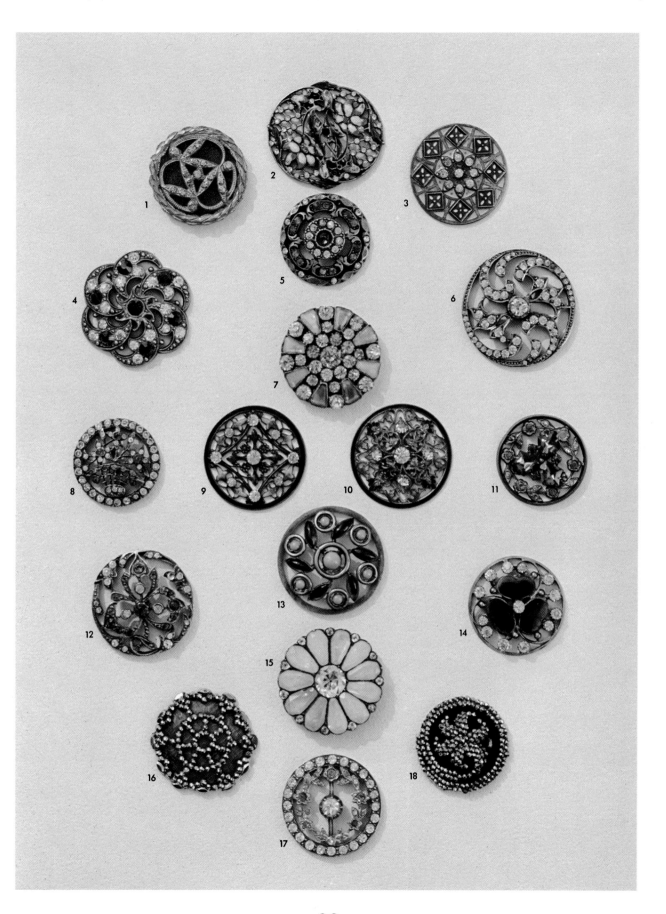

PLATE **30**

Jeweled, Precious, Semi-Precious and Paste

This plate is made up of precious and semi-precious, as well as paste, jewels set in gold of different grades, silver and other metals.

Some jeweled and enameled buttons date from as far back as the Elizabethan period. Buttons 1, 2 and 8 are from this period.

1. Gold with red set.

2. An oval with carved lady's head, set in metal.

3. Ruby-red glass on which is a pearl-trimmed brass flower escutcheon, laid over a radiated metal base, held in place by a sawtoothed bezel with an outer rim trimmed with tiny pearls.

4. An eighteenth century plaque set in silver gilt with 28 rose diamonds in the border.

5. A beautiful button of excellent design and workmanship. The daisylike escutcheon on green glass has a center of massed marcasite; the petals are of pink jewels. There is an engraved copper band around the green glass and a leafy outer rim trimmed with marcasite. All in silver.

6. Faceted ball tiger-eye.

7. There are four parts to this little scalloped button, a jeweled center with a beaded ring between it and the six jewels set on a beaded base to fit the jewels. Gold mounting.

8. Faceted topaz with pinshank.

9, 13, 19, 47. All of these lovely imitation jewel buttons are set in silver; pink, also blue triangle-like sparklers with strass border. Button 47 is all strass in a reticulated base. Button 9 has an opaline cabochon center, surrounded with two circles of green sparklers separated by a circle of faceted opaline glass.

10. Another cut-out silver button trimmed with enamel, baroque pearls and topaz.

11. Another marcasite-trimmed silver button having a latticework pattern over green glass.

12. Faceted smoky topaz.

14, 18, 39. All of these examples of jeweled eighteenth century buttons are set in silver with glass and similar in design. Buttons 14 and 39 have very dark blue glass, 14 with strass trim. And 39 has a center wreath and edge of marcasite. Button 18 has green glass and is strass trimmed.

15. A high-domed button made up of massed garnets.

16. A cameo-carved carnelian set in silver.

17.   Cabochon pink jewels accented with blue pierreries and a sparkler in the center. All set in silver with the number *925* on the shank.

20.   A cut-out design of silver with pink center and four green sparklers and trimmed with marcasite.

21.   Cut-out silver with marcasites and small red cabochon glass center.

22.   Goldstone, bloodstone and lapis lazuli, imitation I'm sure, are set in this attractive gold vest button.

23.   Tiger-eye carved in realistic form of a dog's face and set in gold.

24.   A blue jewel surrounded with a detached ring of marcasite. Set in silver.

25.   Small pearl and turquoise with a center garnet decorate this scalloped and cut-out enamel button.

26 and 28.   The design in both cases is the same except the center jewel in button 26 is set in prongs while the jewel in 28 has been set in a collar. Pearls and turquoise are the jewels used, which were set in silver. Center stones in both are carbuncle (cabochon garnet). Eighteenth or early nineteenth century.

27.   Eight spearhead-shaped jewels, having a paste set between each and surrounding a paste studded center, are set in silver with the back open behind the pink sets. The shank is marked *925*.

29.   Coral and pearls set in a low grade of gold.

30.   Beautiful green moss agate with a brass pinshank and gilt rim. Eighteenth century.

31.   This is silver, trimmed with marcasites with a faceted sparkler in the center.

32.   Green sparklers are flower centers on this cut-out floral button. Hallmarked silver.

33.   Hollow brass button with a solid back and cut-out top trimmed with turquoise, baroque pearl and red jewels.

34.   A baroque pearl centers an enameled disc trimmed with four red sets and placed on a fancy edged button.

35, 36, 37.   The gold collars around the center jewel are loose and can be twisted. On buttons 35 and 37, the collars are over goldstone, which is set in gold. The collar on button 36 is over or above seven red jewels. All of this is displayed on a separate scalloped gold disc to make a frame for the jewels.

38.   The top of this button is very much like the top of 34. Its base is cut out, however, making it lacy in appearance. A rope border finishes it off nicely.

40.   A flowerlike jeweled button with six red petal-shaped sparklers, six square paste jewels between the petals and a paste center. Set in silver. The shank is hallmarked.

41.   A lattice design covers the whole face of this button with paste-trimmed, flowerlike decoration over brilliant green glass.

42.   Lapis lazuli with a pinshank. Early nineteenth century.

43.   A pearl-topped pinshank in a concave, faceted-back amethyst.

44.   Smoky topaz faceted ball.

45.   A cut-out silver button with marcasite and pink oval sparklers.

46.   There is a sheet of copper behind the marcasite trimmed, silver ribbonlike decoration holding two circles of marcasite trimmed silver together. The center is *bleu-de-roi* glass over foil, with an attractive silver escutcheon also trimmed with marcasite.

48.   A faceted coral ball.

PLATE 31

Plant Life

1. Iris cut-out of celluloid.
2. Floral spray showing an insect: sepia-tinted ivory.
3. Crochet over a mold with a gutta-percha chrysanthemum over a velvet background. A thread-back.
4. Pansies, reverse painting on glass with pearl background, set in a drum (deep) collet.
5. Hollow porcelain, floral; crossed swords in center of back.
6. Enamel daisy made in silver.
7. Very thick button of soft paste, hand-painted; circa 1825.
8. Branch with fruit; paint enameled.
9. Spray of flowers escutcheon on conch shell.
10. Lovely carved floral design in amethyst quartz; set in silver. Origin, the Orient.
11. Realistically formed enameled flowers are brazed to a rimmed, lacy back, which is held to a shanked back with four tiny facets.
12. Painted porcelain bachelor-button set in metal.

13. Another hollow porcelain.
14. Pink opaque glass with ivy design.
15. Reverse intaglio rose in glass, painted and set in four-pronged metal collet with center shank on a wire across the back.
16. Engraved iris on lacquered aluminum. At the time these were made, during the latter half of nineteenth century, aluminum was very expensive.
17. Woven fabric chrysanthemum under glass, set in metal much as vest buttons were set.
18 and 24. Carved ivory floral designs.
19. Molded glass rose set in metal.
20. Violet made of enamel set in silver.
21. Lily of the valley. Painted intaglio in high-domed crystal with pearl background, set in metal.
22, 33, 34. Lovely enameled repoussé silver with fine enamel decoration. From the Orient.
23. Floral Satsuma ball.
25. Silver lustre black-glass rose.
26. Brass pansy escutcheon on goldstone.
27. This small transparent enamel with a

chrysanthemum design is set in silver.

28. Parti-enamel iris on cut-out metal trimmed with faceted steels.

29. A tulip on porcelain; Copenhagen with Three Rivers mark.

30. Eighteenth century needlework, combined with gold and colored foil, was used to make this flower.

31. Silver lustre flowers on brown-colored black glass.

32. Pierced metal with hazelnut design.

35. Another metal button with nut design.

36. Horn base with partial wreath of wild roses.

37. Wooden button with vegetable-ivory grapes attached to the back with screws.

38. Pierced metal of leaves with blued steels clustered to form fruit.

39. Vegetable-ivory cherries pinned to the back of a composition button.

40. Silver tulip with hallmark in edge. Bone back.

PLATE 32

Plant Life

Here is another plate of buttons illustrating plant life, which shows my penchant for this category. I prefer identifiable plants rather than conventionalized ones. Yet, even though plants may be conventional, I will find a place in my collection for those which display particular beauty and/or fine workmanship.

1. A lovely wild rose. Two-color pierced metal.

2. A reverse painting on glass with pearl background set in a brass drum collet.

3. Nasturtium. This is a hard flower to find on a button; used here as a bonnet on a girl's head.

4. Carved pearl daisy.

5. Art nouveau tulip, tinted and paste trimmed. Two-color metal.

6, 7, 9, 10. Beautiful examples of basse-taille enamel, made on silver. A rose, iris, violets and chrysanthemum.

8, 11, 13. These are examples of lovely glass, a lacy tulip; a clear glass silvered poppy; and an enameled daisy used as an escutcheon on crystal glass.

12. A realistically made water lily of metal set in a wide ring of metal. The buds are of green glass.

14, 15, 16, 17. A pansy, clematis, tulip and wild rose. These are Copenhagen, all with Three Rivers mark.

18. Brass cut-out carnation trimmed with paste.

19. The flower heads on this flat, painted metal button are painted over small pearl slices which give a lovely lustre.

20. Black glass with gold-filled lines and painted flowers, set in metal with faceted steels.

21. Brass floral design inlaid in amber glass.

22. Openwork, two-color metal thistle.

23, 25, 27, 28. Beautifully painted flowers on ivory under glass, set in metal, tin backs. Eighteenth century. Flower subjects are rare for this period.

24. Iris is shown here in plique-à-jour enamel.

26. Two-color, cut-out metal poppy.

29. Silver lustre black glass wild rose.

Realistics and Geometric Shapes

1. Human head of black glass.

2, 4, 6, 10. Pearl-trimmed brass buttons of a pocket knife, gun, scissors and a key.

3. Porcelain ball with rose decoration.

5. Owl head of black glass.

7. Enameled flower head.

8. Scarab of transparent enamel.

9. Brass slipper.

11. Ivory with faceted steels.

12. Butterfly of plique-à-jour enamel.

13. Porcelain ball with fruit decoration.

14. An insect made entirely of faceted steels.

15. A lovely jade and kingfisher-feather fastener.

16. Black glass dog's head with red eyes and a silver collar pinned to a flat metal back of the same shape.

17. Black glass lady's head with a silver crown; same treatment as button 16.

18. Another button with kingfisher-feather trim.

19. Cat's head of quartz.

20. Paisley shape of black glass.

21. Pearl ear of corn.

22. Carved wood dog's head with glass eyes.

23. Mirrored red glass on metal back of the same shape.

24. Pearl pansy face of smoky pearl layers, carved in light to dark.

25 and 26. A dog's head and a leaf; both black glass.

27. Satsuma ball with butterfly decoration.

28. Snail shell was used for this dog's head. Glass eyes.

29. Carved ivory hibiscus. A curved needle is needed for securing this button to fabric.

30. Egyptian mummy of silver.

31 and 41. Both marked Wedgwood; both black basalt. Each is set in silver with a cross-bar open back.

32. Opaque glass dog's head.

33. Pair of shoes of horn.

34. Lovely brass basket of flowers with colored stones for the flowers. The diamond-shaped silver base is trimmed with marcasite.

35 and 37.   A hoof and a scallop shell. Solid tortoise.

36.   Large ivory die with faceted steels used for numbering the sides.

38.   Carved, elongated scallop shell with young woman's head in center. Lava.

39.   Flower head of ivory.

40.   Carved jade lotus flower.

42.   Silver iris.

PLATE 34

Paisley Designs

These paisley design buttons have been made of many different materials.

1 and 3. Metals.

4 and 20. Opaque glass.

6 and 8. Under glass.

7. Mosaic.

9. Black glass with a celluloid background, set in metal.

10. Steel-cup.

11. Pinna shell.

12. Fabric set in metal.

13, 15, 23. Enamels.

14. Pearl.

16 and 18. Inlays.

19. Clear glass.

21. Lacy glass.

PLATE 35

Heads

1. This portrait is of Marie Antoinette. Originally, there were more in this set of painted heads, all identified on the back.

2. Miniature on ivory, under glass and set in a fancy silver gilt rim, trimmed with pearls.

3. *Pâté-sur-pâté* (paste-on-paste) porcelain.

4. A seed-pearl-trimmed silver bow and rim add to the beauty of this miniature on ivory.

5. Hand-finished decal on porcelain.

6. Painted enamel head with heavy encrusted gold edge and paste border set in white metal. Marked *Paris*.

7. Art nouveau head with blue plique-à-jour trim.

8. Classical head carved from shaded pearl, dark to light. Pronged paste forms a complete circle around the head, but is separated from it with spokes holding the ring of paste to a shanked flat back.

9, 24, 27. Transfers on porcelain, set in metal.

10. This is a porcelain button with a lovely bisque head. The rest of the button is glazed.

Painted black border.

11. Eighteenth century die-struck copper Colonial, with enamel painted ground.

12. Very clear nice lithograph, under glass and set in metal.

13. Charlotte Corday, a lithograph under isinglass, set in an imitation tortoise celluloid.

14. Miniature on ivory with paste and blue sparkler borders.

15. Lithograph set in a fancy white metal frame.

16. Seneca, from a set of famous Romans, painted in the grisaille manner on ivory, under glass, set in metal with ivory back.

17. Head of matte enamel set in white metal with border of paste.

18. Produced in same manner as button 16. There are two profiles on this "one" head, so if the button gets turned upside down by chance, it still has a recognizable picture.

19. Parti-enamel on brass, with faceted steels for trim.

20. A signed miniature, under glass, set in

metal with pronged paste.

21.   Classical head carved from a conch shell. Set in metal with faceted steel border.

22.   Brass head of Mercury with screenlike background filled in with faceted steels. Rope border.

23.   From the eighteenth century; undoubtedly Wedgwood jasper cameo. Set in brass.

25.   Carved smoky pearl.

26.   Decal on porcelain set in metal with paste border. Late nineteenth century.

28.   Another lithograph set in celluloid, framed with a brass rope ring studded with steels. Steels also decorate the ivy-leaf incised border.

29.   Miniature on ivory, under glass, set in a fancy cut-out metal, paste trimmed border.

Buttons 13 and 28 as well as some on Plate 19 are what I have always called solid celluloids, as they are not formed from a thin sheet of celluloid. I have many of them and they are most interesting, I think, and completely different from the many celluloid buttons which are set in metal frames.

PLATE 36

Oriental

The subject matter of this plate pertains to the Orient. The materials are assorted.

1. Gesso work on flat steel. Figure of a man.

2. A lovely lady, reverse painting on glass with a delicately woven border of gold-colored wire, punctuated with small balls of metal. Outer edge slightly scalloped.

3. A basse-taille enamel dragon set in silver.

4. Satsuma with overall butterfly design.

5. Chinese man standing in front of a house. Pressed wood.

6. Carved and tinted ivory of a woman and a man.

7. Black glass pagoda.

8. Porcelain ball of a dragon with flowerlike top on a pinshank.

9. Gold Mandarin ball.

10. Satsuma peonies.

11. A steel cup showing two figures.

12. Opaque glass scene from *The Mikado.*

13. A junk inlaid in a thin layer of tortoise on a horn base.

14. A country scene in black and white

makes a frame for a center design of a seated man blowing on a long reed. Gold background. Set in metal with fancy prongs.

15. A scene on tole.

16. Cut-out metal, with a lady holding an enamel fan.

17. Hexagonal pearl with one of the happiness characters.

18. Two-color metal boat scene.

19. An Oriental man playing a lute. Metal on pearl.

20. Basse-taille enamel of iris set in silver.

21. Chinese man with fan of pressed horn.

22. Jade bat.

23. Jade with brass pinshank.

24. Satsuma lady set in silver.

25. Silk toggle.

Old Paperweights

1. A faceted, frosted paperweight.

2, 5, 6, 7, 8, 9, 10, 14, 15, 17, 19, 26, 35, 36, 39, 40. All of these buttons were blown in a mold, thus producing a top design.

12. Set-up has flowers and an animal on a latticino red base.

16. White latticino lines on black glass base.

18. A canary-color sulphide head.

21 and 40. Have flat tops but shaped sides.

33. A crackle-glass paperweight.

36. A fine floral set-up.

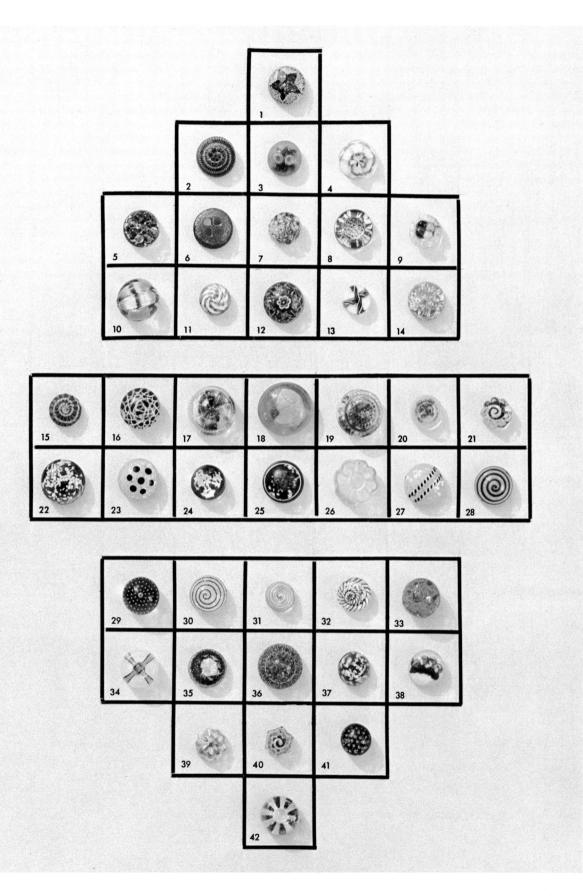

Modern Paperweights, After 1918

1, 16, 48. Made by Winfield Rutter.

2 and 3. Made by William Iorio.

4 through 7, 19 through 26, 28 through 35, 45, 49 through 54. Made by Charles Kaziun.

8 through 15, 17 and 18, 37 through 44. Made by Thura Erickson. Button 8 is a frog. Button 9 has a snake figure, and 18 has a turtle figure.

27 and 36. Made by Jacques Israel.

In checking over this group I find I have neglected to include some of Francis X. Weinman's very nice examples. Charles Kaziun is our best artisan today. William Iorio is still perfecting his technique, while the other three artisans, as well as Mr. Weinman, have gone from our midst.

PLATE 39

Lacy Glass

This plate of lacy glass is unique because quite a few of the buttons shown have colored bodies instead of clear with painted backs.

8 and 9. There are also two clear lacy shown.

These buttons have been called "lacy" be cause they resemble lacy Sandwich glass. Research has shown that Sandwich made only small centers, which were used by button manufacturers in making waistcoat or vest buttons.

39

PLATE 40

Cuff Buttons

These cuff buttons belonged to Mr. Ertell, and this is but one of two trays he had. After his passing I broke up one of the trays to give sons and grandsons their choices. Mr. Ertell wore pairs from both trays except for the very large pearl heads shown on this plate, buttons 4 and 5.

The materials show up very well in the plate except, perhaps, the papier-maché pair, buttons 7 and 9.

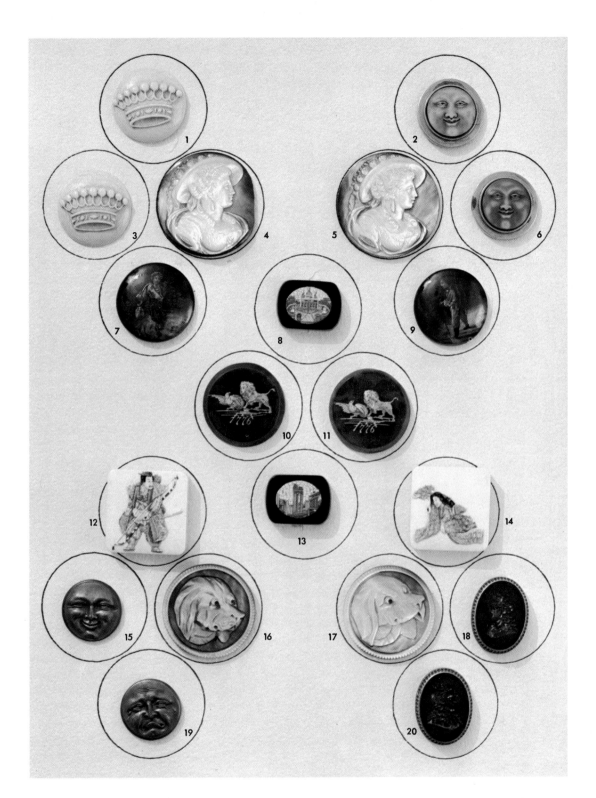

40

PLATE 41

Moderns, Since 1918

1, 5, 7, 9. Examples of modern damascene.

2. A translucent enamel set in metal.

3. Carved, pigmented ivory monkey from a zodiac set.

4. Modern damascene.

6. An enamel button, frog on a lily pad.

8. Enamel dragon, 1918.

10. Hexagonal silver button, partially trimmed with transparent enamel. I firmly believe that this and the enamel dragon and frog are of Chinese orgin. It's also possible that the frog and the hexagonal enamel are older than others on this plate, but some collectors say "no."

19. Cats of Satsuma ware.

The rest of the buttons are Satsuma, some, such as the cats, made to order for individual customers. All but the enamels are from Japan.

PLATE 42

Moderns, Since 1918

1 through 6, 9.   Arita porcelain, Japan.

7, 11, 14, 16.   Wood inlay; made by the Indian artist, Matawala.

8.   Three monkeys, square, Arita porcelain, Japan.

10.   Gold wire cock; made by Matawala of India.

12.   Ivory with elephant border; made by Matawala of India.

13.   Hibiscus, made of ivory.

15.   Crab, zodiac sign of India.

17.   Bird made of feathers on pearl under glass.

18.   Swan, transparent enamel on silver.

19.   Alligator, zodiac sign of India.

20.   Scorpion, zodiac sign of India.

21.   See-saw, a Kate Greenaway design, painted enamel.

22.   Square button painted in the Persian manner, ivory.

23.   Oblong scene, incised and pigmented. Set in typical Chinese mounting.

24.   Round button painted in the Persian

manner, pearl.

    25.   Bachelor-button painted on porcelain. One of a set of twenty done by H. F. Meyer in 1942. Marked on back of each button. Only a few sets were made.

    26 and 27.   Carved floral pearls of Japanese origin.

    28.   Goldfish, inlay in ivory, Japanese.

PLATE 43

Moderns, Since 1918

1. A gold miner panning for gold with his faithful burro companion.

2. A colorful basket, under glass and set in metal.

3. Lacy glass center with much pearl and paste jewel trim.

4. Semi-precious stone insect. Experts on Indian work believe this button is of such origin.

5. Made by John Harris; dated January, 1971.

6. "Imitation Wedgwood," should we call it, or fine ceramic work by Marie LaBarre Bennett? Subjects are Alexander and Olympius.

7. Cut-off corners on this extra-large square button do not make it appear any smaller. Striking metal head with paste trim on celluloid.

8. The bear is the symbol of the State of California, and this one in high relief is a handsome specimen. Signed *J-Lu.G. Button Co. Sterling.*

9. Insect escutcheon on pearl.

10. Butterfly wings were used to make this scene, under glass and set in metal.

11. Heart-shaped Toledo ware.

12. Another escutcheon on pearl of a clown decorated with red paste.

13. Indian turquoise in silver: a beautiful piece.

14. This certainly wouldn't be very practical as a button, but it was a sample I bought from one of the button suppliers.

15. Woven straw by a Nootka Indian, Canada.

16. An undistinguished but very pretty button.

17 and 18. Enamels, from Limoges, France. Some of the enamel is made thicker, giving a realistic appearance.

19. A charming enamel scene of a courting couple, set in metal.

20. Carved pearl deer, from Palestine.

21. Dog escutcheon on an extra-large abalone base.

22. White metal picture button of a woman spinning.

23 and 26. Watch-crystal types made by Theodore Gates of State College, Pennsylvania. They are signed and dated. The head is a Godey print from one of the magazines.

24. Enamel figure with imitation pierreries, attributed to Austria.

25. Floral needlepoint, set in metal, Austrian.

Composed in Linofilm Baskerville with Perpetua
by Ruttle, Shaw & Wetherill
Printed by Pearl Pressman Liberty
Color separations by Infinity Color

Designed by Gwendolyn O. England